Dinosaur A-Z

T0015748

Written by Simon Mugford
Designed by Jo Rigg

priddy books
big ideas for little people

A is for Allosaurus

I'm a meat-eater and I like to go hunting with my **friends.** I am huge, scary and I have very, very **sharp** teeth. I like to eat other dinosaurs, especially **big** ones with long necks.

Say my name: al-oh-SAWR-us

B is for
crocodile-like jaws
Dinosaur height: 10 ft
My name is Baryonyx, which means 'heavy claw.' I like to eat smaller dinosaurs but my favorite food is fish. I catch them with my claws and then chew them up with my jagged teeth!
96 sharp, jagged teeth
strong claws useful for catching fish
Baryonyx
Say my name: BAH-ree-ON-iks

My name means 'hollow-boned,' and I am **small** and light. This means I can **run** very fast, which is useful for chasing things to eat and getting away from those who want to eat **me!**

Say my name: SEE-low-FIE-sis

D is for Diplodocus

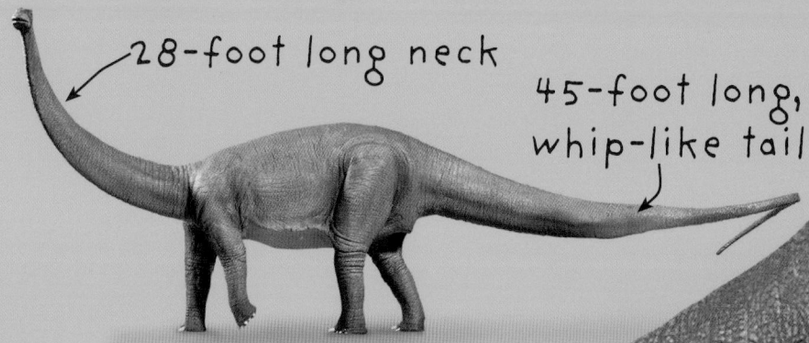

small head

big, heavy feet

I am one of the longest dinosaurs that ever lived. I eat plants, but I can't chew very well, so I swallow huge stones that mash up the food in my enormous stomach.

Say my name: di-PLOD-uh-kus

E is for Euoplocephalus

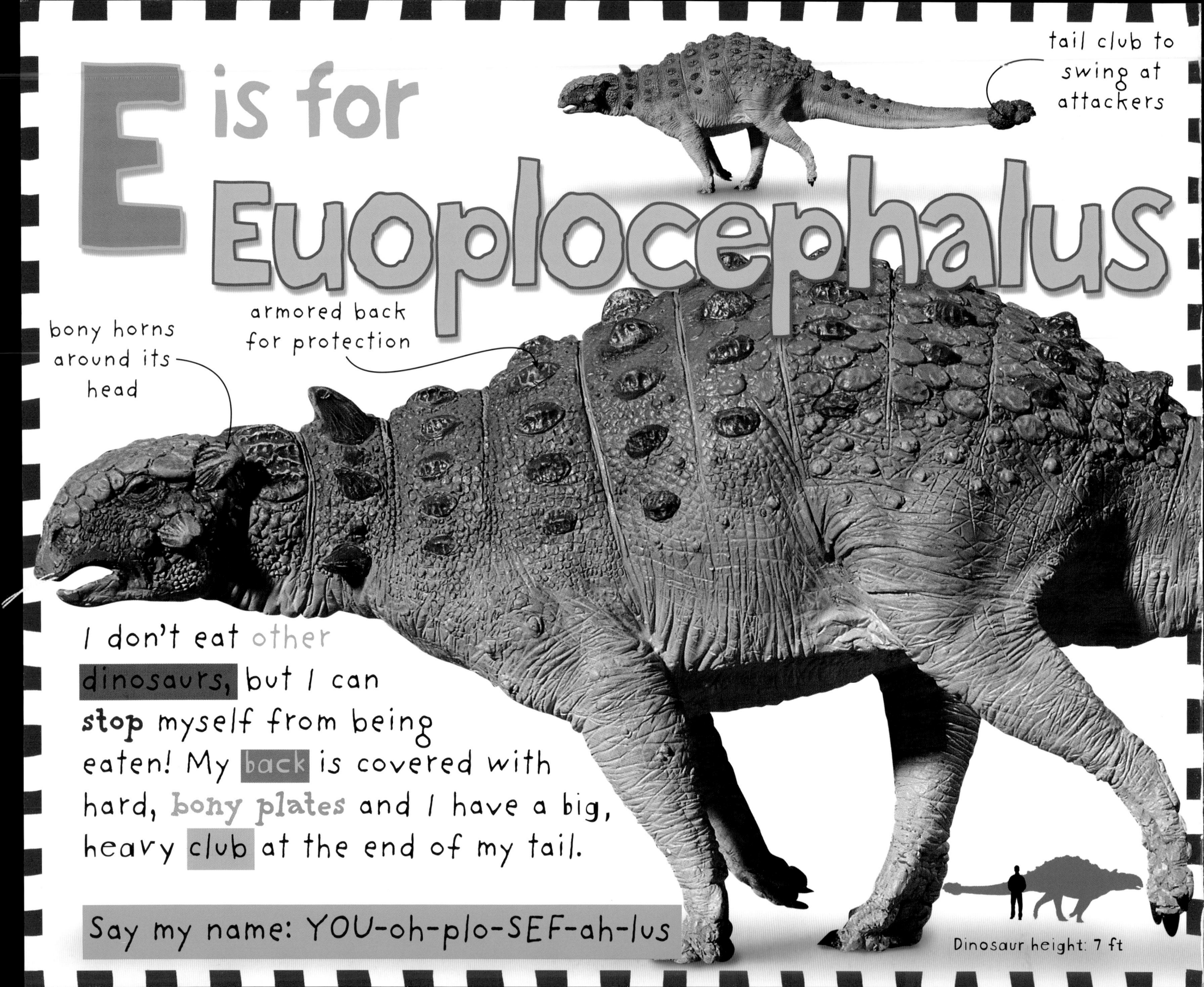

I don't eat other dinosaurs, but I can **stop** myself from being eaten! My back is covered with hard, **bony plates** and I have a big, heavy club at the end of my tail.

Say my name: YOU-oh-plo-SEF-ah-lus

Dinosaur height: 7 ft

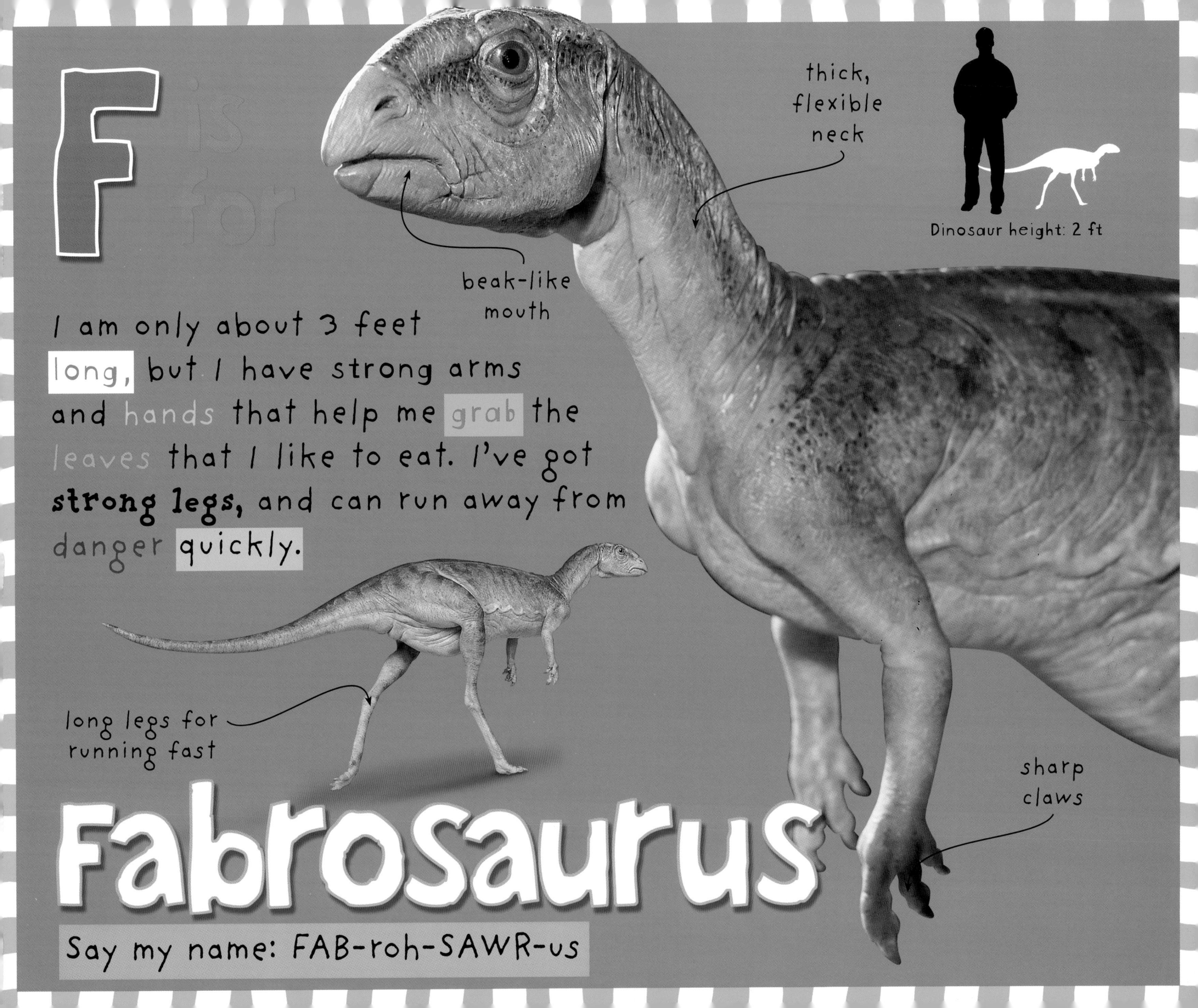
F is for
thick, flexible neck
Dinosaur height: 2 ft
beak-like mouth
I am only about 3 feet long, but I have strong arms and hands that help me grab the leaves that I like to eat. I've got **strong legs,** and can run away from danger quickly.
long legs for running fast
sharp claws
Fabrosaurus
Say my name: FAB-roh-SAWR-us

G is for
Gravitholus
bashing heads
Dinosaur height: 15 ft
long, stiff, heavy tail
We have very thick skulls, and that's why the other dinosaurs call us 'bone-heads.' We like to charge into each other headfirst, but sometimes it gives us a headache!
clawed feet
thick, rounded skull
Say my name: GRA-vith-OH-lus

H is for
duck-like beak
Dinosaur height: 20 ft
I'm often called 'duck bill' because my mouth looks like a beak. I have very small, flat teeth inside my cheeks, which I use to chew the plants that I like to eat.
flexible neck
Hadrosaurus
Say my name: HAD-roh-SAWR-us

I is for
sharp thumb spike
sharp, toothless beak
Wherever I go, I always meet other Iguanodons because there are lots of us around! I use the bony spike on my thumb to defend myself if someone starts a fight.
powerful legs
Iguanodon
Say my name: Ig-WAN-oh-DON
Dinosaur height: 18 ft

J is for
Janenschia
I'm about 80 feet long – pretty cool, right? With these bony plates on my back, I don't have to worry about predators. I eat a lot and I stand on my rear legs to reach the leaves in very high trees.
long neck for reaching food in trees
tough, bony plates across the back
very strong legs to support its weight
30-foot long tail
Dinosaur height: 56 ft
Say my name: yah-NEN-chee-ah

K is for Kentrosaurus

Say my name: KEN-troh-SAWR-us

bony plates

sharp spikes

My name means **'prickly reptile.'** I **guess** that's because of these spikes along my **back** and **tail** – they are there to protect me. I have a very small brain so I'm not the smartest **dinosaur.**

small head and brain

Dinosaur height: 12 ft

L is for
walks on four legs
head crest
My name means 'slender-horned face.' I'm about 6 feet long and I have this really cool-looking head crest and a little horned beak to bite my food.
beak
Dinosaur height: 2½ ft
Leptoceratops
Say my name: LEP-to-SEH-ruh-tops

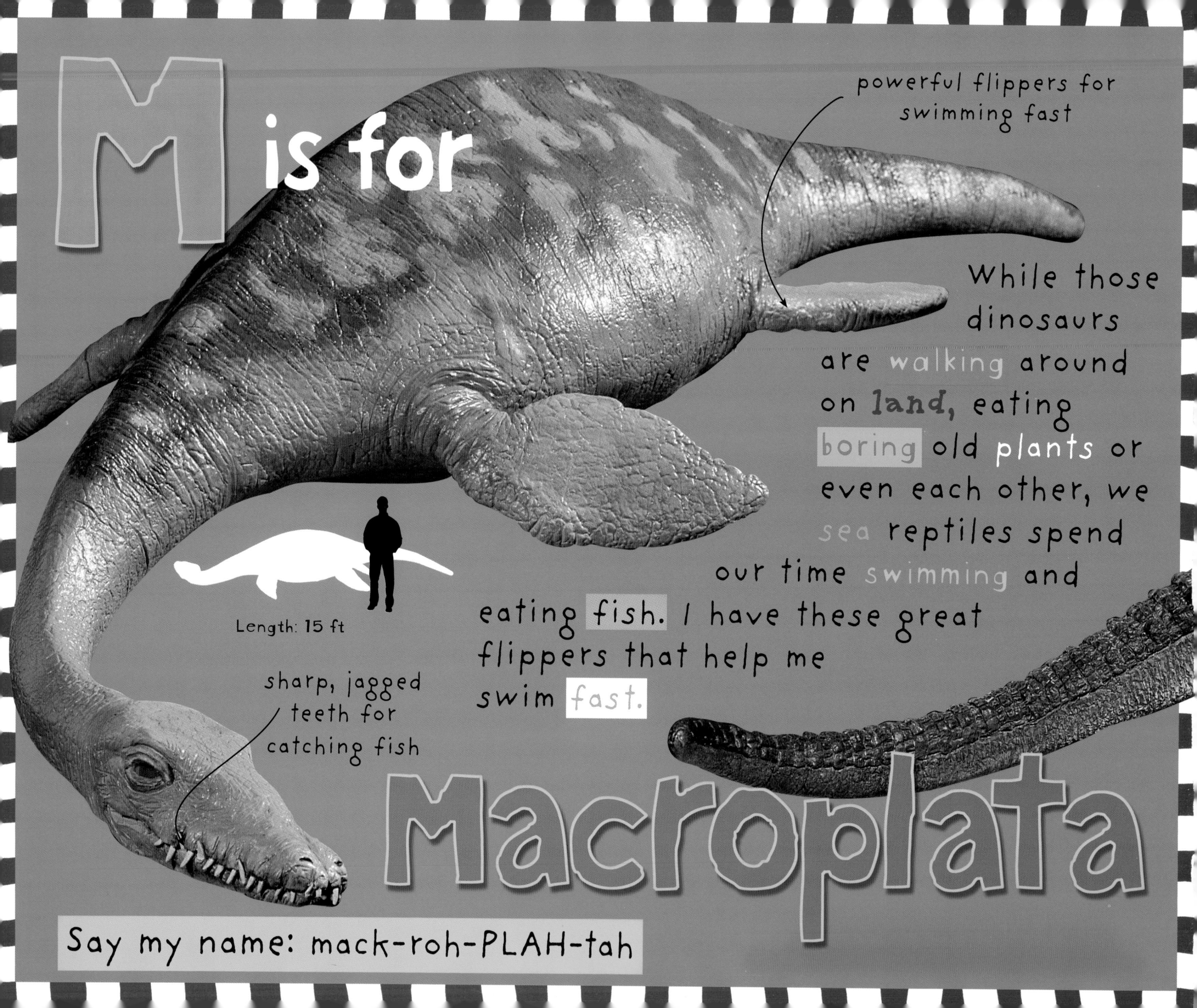
M is for
powerful flippers for swimming fast
While those dinosaurs are walking around on land, eating boring old plants or even each other, we sea reptiles spend our time swimming and eating fish. I have these great flippers that help me swim fast.
Length: 15 ft
sharp, jagged teeth for catching fish
Macroplata
Say my name: mack-roh-PLAH-tah

N is for Nodosaurus

My **armor-plating** has given me my name – it means 'lumpy reptile.' Those knobbly plates on my back are really tough and it takes a lot to hurt me. I eat plants that are close to the ground.

Say my name: NODE-oh-SAWR-us

O is for
long, spiny sail along its back
Dinosaur height: 15 ft
The 'sail' on my back is very helpful – I let the sun shine on it to warm me up. To cool down, I turn the sail into the wind and let it blow on my back.
four fingers and a spiked thumb
Ouranosaurus
three-toed feet
Say my name: oo-RAHN-oh-SAWR-us

P is for

long, hollow head crest

knobbly-textured skin

short, stiff tail

It may look **weird**, but that long tube on top of my head comes in useful. I can blow through it to make a really **loud** noise and warn my friends if I see anything **dangerous.**

Dinosaur height: 13 ft

Parasaurolophus

Say my name: PAR-ah-sawr-OL-oh-fus

Q is for Quetzalcoatlus

I am a **flying** reptile that **lived** at the same time as the dinosaurs. I am the biggest of my **kind** and the largest creature ever to fly. I like to eat fish, but sometimes I scavenge for scraps of meat.

Say my name: KET-sal-koh-AT-lus

R is for Riojasaurus
small head with large eyes
long neck
I am one of the oldest of all the plant-eating dinosaurs and the first to have a long neck. I have big, heavy, strong legs and my bones are very solid and thick. I am about 36 feet long.
Dinosaur height: 17 ft
15-foot long tail
Say my name: ree-OH-ha-SAWR-us

S is for
very large eyes
Dinosaur height: 7 ft
I am a very smart dinosaur and I have very good eyesight, which helps me when I'm out hunting for food. People also call me 'Troodon,' but I prefer Stenonychosaurus.
bony spikes along its back
long, stiff tail
sharp claws
stenonychosaurus
Say my name: ste-NON-ik-oh-SAWR-us

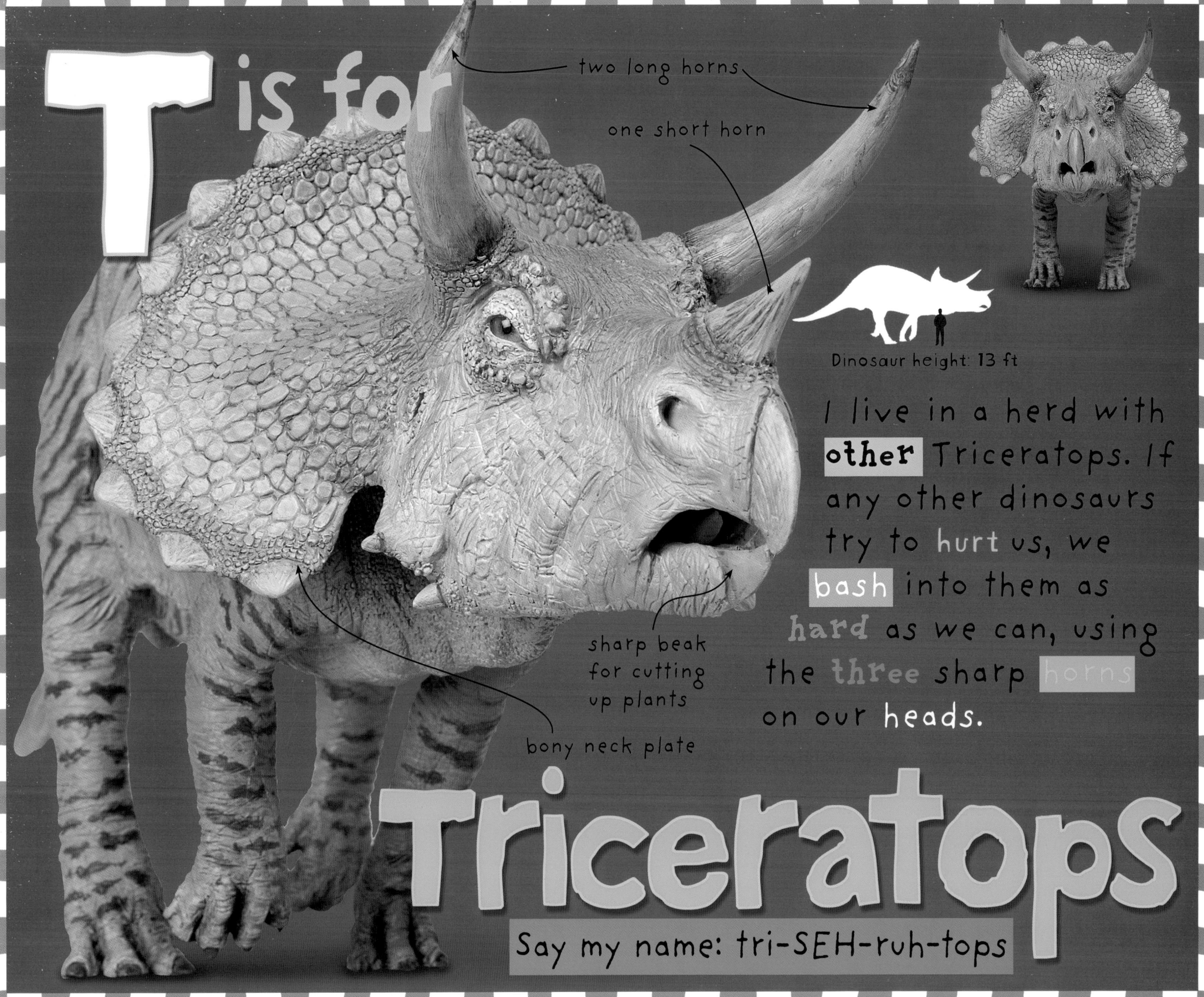
T is for
two long horns
one short horn
Dinosaur height: 13 ft
I live in a herd with other Triceratops. If any other dinosaurs try to hurt us, we bash into them as hard as we can, using the three sharp horns on our heads.
sharp beak for cutting up plants
bony neck plate
Triceratops
Say my name: tri-SEH-ruh-tops

Say my name: UL-trah-SAWR-oss
U is for
Ultrasauros
Scientists first called me Ultrasauros but I am now known as Supersaurus. I like both names, and I think you'll agree, I am most definitely a supersized dinosaur! Dinosaurs like me are among the biggest creatures ever to have lived on Earth.
very long neck
bony head crest
small mouth and teeth
long tail
Dinosaur height: 50 ft

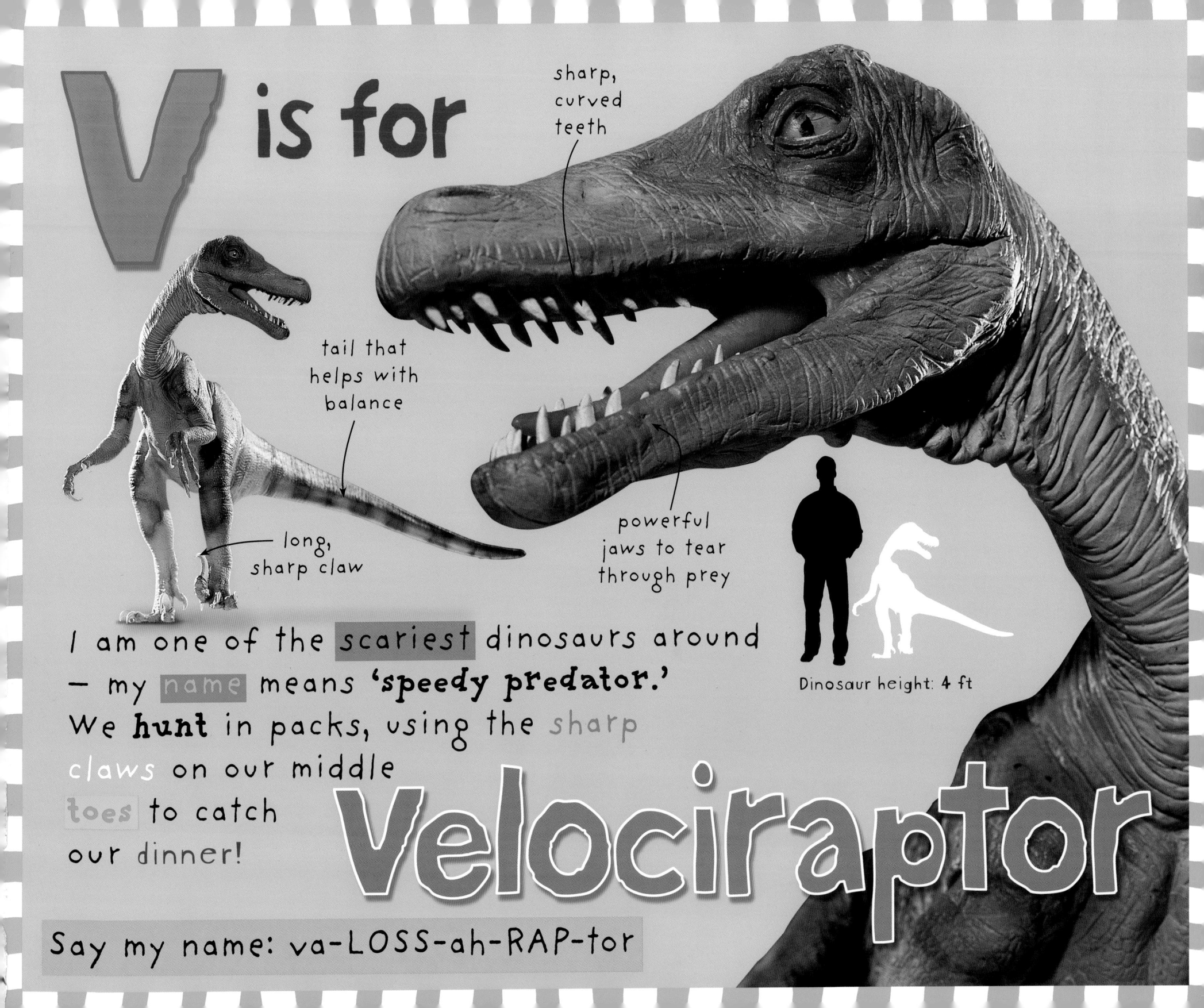
V is for
sharp, curved teeth
tail that helps with balance
long, sharp claw
powerful jaws to tear through prey
Dinosaur height: 4 ft
I am one of the scariest dinosaurs around – my name means 'speedy predator.' We hunt in packs, using the sharp claws on our middle toes to catch our dinner!
Velociraptor
Say my name: va-LOSS-ah-RAP-tor

W is for
hard, flat skull
Dinosaur height: 2 ft
short arms
stiff tail and bulky body
I am a lot smaller than my crazy cousin Gravitholus, and my head isn't quite as thick, but I still like to use it to play head-banging games with my friends!
Wannanosaurus
Say my name: wah-NAN-oh-SAWR-us

X is for
knobbly back and neck
two horns above the eyes
long, stiff tail
strong legs
Dinosaur height: 22 ft
I am a big, meat-eating dinosaur. Those little horns above my eyes and the spikes on my back might seem a little strange, but I don't care – they make me look scary!
Xenotarsosaurus
Say my name: zeen-oh-TAR-soh-SAWR-us

Y is for
Dinosaur height: 18 ft
bony plates along back and tail
I use the plates on my back to warm myself by facing them toward the sun and cool down by turning away from it.
I protect myself with these really sharp spikes on my tail.
small head
Yingshanosaurus
Say my name: YING-shan-oh-SAWR-us

Z is for
Zephyrosaurus
Dinosaur height: 4 ft
strong jaws, with teeth in the cheeks
I am small, I eat plants and I can run pretty fast. My long tail helps me to keep my balance, and that makes running quickly a lot easier. I really like my name – it means 'west wind reptile.'
five-fingered hands
long tail
long rear legs
Say my name: ZEF-ih-roh-SAWR-us

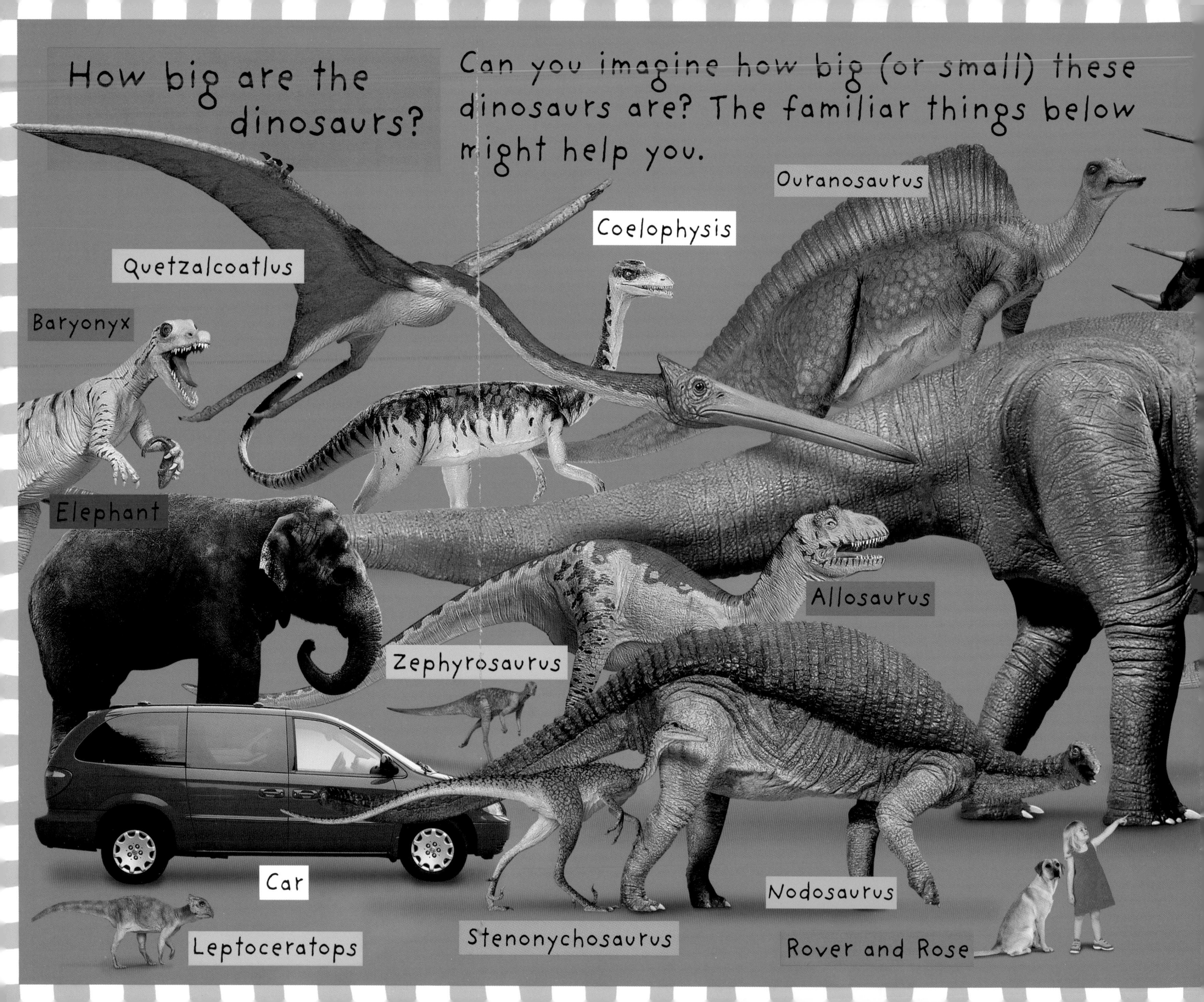
How big are the dinosaurs?
Can you imagine how big (or small) these dinosaurs are? The familiar things below might help you.
Ouranosaurus
Coelophysis
Quetzalcoatlus
Baryonyx
Elephant
Allosaurus
Zephyrosaurus
Car
Nodosaurus
Leptoceratops
Stenonychosaurus
Rover and Rose